FROM DREAMS TO RICHES

INSPIRING JOURNEYS OF INDIAN ENTREPRENEURS

ARITRA MANNA

Contents

Foreword   *v*

Preface   *vii*

Acknowledgements   *ix*

Prologue   *xi*

Introduction of the Author, Aritra Manna   *xiii*

1. The Landscape Of Entrepreneurship In India   1

2. The Mindset Of A Millionaire   4

3. Financial Literacy: The Key To Success   8

4. Identifying Opportunities In The Market   13

5. Building A Business Plan   19

6. Funding Your Venture   24

7. Navigating Legal And Regulatory Frameworks   28

8. Marketing Strategies For Growth   32

9. Technology As A Catalyst For Success   36

10. Building A Strong Team: The Foundation Of Entrepreneurial   39
    Success

11. The DNA Of A Successful Entrepreneur   42

12. The Success Story Of Maa Tara Jewellers   47

13. YouTubers As Entrepreneurs   52

14. Built By Grit: The Rise Of Madan Karande And The Balaji Legacy 56

15. Old Mumbai Ice Creams   64

16. Chapter:15 My Success Story   67

The Power of Persistence   71

Impact Beyond Wealth   73

The Journey Ahead   75

Foreword

Entrepreneurship is not merely about creating businesses; it is about transforming dreams into reality, shaping ideas into meaningful impact, and turning challenges into opportunities.

As I pen the foreword to From Dreams to Riches: Inspiring Journeys of Indian Entrepreneurs, I reflect on the transformative power of vision, resilience, and the entrepreneurial spirit.

This book is a labor of love, born from my deep fascination with the stories of individuals who dared to dream boldly and pursued those dreams with relentless passion.

Growing up in a family rooted in business, I have witnessed firsthand the grit, sacrifice, and determination required to build something extraordinary. Watching my father, Vishwajit Manna, and my uncle, Prasenjit Manna, transform Maa Tara Jewellers into a symbol of trust and excellence profoundly shaped my understanding of entrepreneurship and inspired me to explore the journeys of others who have walked similar paths.

Each story in this book is unique, yet they all share powerful common threads — perseverance, creativity, resilience, and the courage to take risks. These values are not only essential for building successful businesses but are also fundamental to living a life of purpose and impact.

From humble beginnings to landmark achievements, these entrepreneurs overcame countless obstacles with unwavering belief in their dreams, offering lessons that extend far beyond the world of business.

From Dreams to Riches is more than a collection of success stories; it is a tribute to the indomitable entrepreneurial spirit that drives innovation and progress across India.

It serves as a reminder that success is not confined to the privileged few, but is attainable for anyone willing to embrace hard work, learn from failure, and persist through adversity.

As you turn the pages, I hope you find inspiration in these journeys. Whether you are an aspiring entrepreneur, an established professional, or simply someone seeking motivation, may these stories awaken the boundless potential within you.

To the dreamers who dare to create and to the achievers who inspire others to believe — this book is for you.

Warm regards,
Aritra Manna
Author of From Dreams to Riches: Inspiring Journeys of Indian Entrepreneurs

Preface

From Dreams to Riches: Inspiring Journeys of Indian Entrepreneurs is more than a book; it is a reflection of the determination, innovation, and resilience that define the true spirit of entrepreneurship.

The inspiration for this work stems from my personal journey — growing up in a family that transformed a simple dream into a lasting legacy.

Watching my father, Vishwajit Manna, and my uncle, Prasenjit Manna, build Maa Tara Jewellers from the ground up instilled in me a deep appreciation for the grit, discipline, and perseverance it takes to succeed in the world of business.

As I ventured into entrepreneurship myself, I realized the profound influence that stories of perseverance and triumph have on shaping an individual's mindset.

This realization motivated me to explore and share the journeys of other remarkable entrepreneurs who have turned their aspirations into thriving ventures.

Each story in this book stands as a testament to the transformative power of vision, determination, and relentless pursuit of goals.

It is my hope that these stories will inspire others to pursue their ambitions with unwavering passion and courage.

Writing this book has been a journey of learning and personal growth.

It has deepened my understanding of the entrepreneurial process and reinforced my belief that true success is not simply about reaching a destination, but about embracing the challenges along the way and evolving through them.

This book is dedicated to the dreamers, the doers, and to anyone seeking inspiration to chase their aspirations.

It is a celebration of the entrepreneurial spirit that drives innovation, builds communities, and shapes the future of our society.

I am deeply grateful to the entrepreneurs whose stories are featured in these pages for generously sharing their journeys with me.

I am equally indebted to my family — especially my parents and my uncle — whose unwavering support, encouragement, and belief in my vision have been my greatest pillars of strength.

I hope this book serves as a beacon of motivation for all who read it.

May it remind you that no dream is too distant, no obstacle insurmountable, and no goal beyond reach when pursued with passion, perseverance, and purpose.

Warm regards,
Aritra Manna
Author of From Dreams to Riches: Inspiring Journeys of Indian Entrepreneurs

Acknowledgements

Writing From Dreams to Riches: Inspiring Journeys of Indian Entrepreneurs has been a deeply rewarding and transformative experience. I am profoundly grateful to everyone who has supported, encouraged, and inspired me throughout this journey.

First and foremost, I would like to express my heartfelt thanks to my parents, Vishwajit Manna and Madhumitha Manna.
Your unwavering love, belief, and endless encouragement have been the foundation upon which my dreams have been built.
To my uncle, Prasenjit Manna — your wisdom, dedication, and constant support have been instrumental in shaping my understanding of perseverance, leadership, and resilience.

A special thanks to Shri Balaji Public School and Sanjay Ghodawat International School, the institutions where my academic journey began and continues to flourish.
The lessons learned, values instilled, and mentors encountered during these formative years have significantly influenced both my personal and professional growth.
To all my teachers, guides, and mentors — thank you for lighting the path ahead and for helping me believe in my dreams.

I am deeply indebted to the entrepreneurs whose incredible stories are featured in this book.
Your journeys of determination, innovation, and success have been a source of immense inspiration not just for me, but for all who will read these pages. Thank you for entrusting me with your experiences and allowing me to share them with the world.

To my friends, family, and supporters — your encouragement, patience, and positivity have been the steady wind beneath my wings.
Your belief in me, even during moments of doubt, helped turn a vision into reality.

Lastly, I am grateful to every dreamer, doer, and believer who continues to inspire the world through action and passion.
This book is a tribute to your spirit.

Thank you for being part of this journey.

Prologue

In the heart of India, where dreams are as vast as the sky and the journey to success is often long and challenging, there exists a profound truth — entrepreneurship is the engine that drives the nation forward.

From Dreams to Riches: Inspiring Journeys of Indian Entrepreneurs is a celebration of this indomitable spirit, showcasing the stories of individuals who transformed their dreams into thriving enterprises against all odds.

This book is not merely a collection of success stories; it is an exploration of the grit, resilience, and relentless determination that define the entrepreneurial spirit of India.

These are individuals who started with little more than an idea, a vision, and an unshakable belief that they could create something greater than themselves.

Through every challenge, every setback, and every obstacle, they moved forward — understanding that the road to success is rarely linear, but always worth traveling.

Entrepreneurship, as I have discovered through my own journey, is about far more than financial success.

It is about creating value, solving real-world problems, and contributing meaningfully to the greater good.

As a young entrepreneur myself, I have been profoundly inspired by the men and women featured in this book — individuals who have not only built successful businesses but have also uplifted communities, created opportunities, and shaped entire industries.

The stories within these pages are diverse, yet interconnected.

From the seed of an idea to the realization of a vision, the path to success is different for everyone.

Yet, passion, persistence, and an unwavering commitment to their goals bind these journeys together.

It is my hope that their experiences will inspire you to embark on your own path, to believe in the power of your dreams, and to know that success is possible, regardless of where you begin.

As you read through these accounts of triumphs and trials, may you find the motivation and encouragement to pursue your aspirations.

The journey of an entrepreneur is undoubtedly challenging — but as these stories reveal, it is also deeply transformative and incredibly rewarding.

This book is a tribute to those who dared to dream — and through hard work, vision, and perseverance — turned their dreams into lasting legacies.

I invite you to step into their world, to draw inspiration from their journeys, and to ignite your own path toward success.

With hope and gratitude,
Aritra Manna

Introduction Of The Author, Aritra Manna

Aritra Manna is a dynamic entrepreneurial, visionary leader, and budding author from Ichalkaranji, Maharashtra. Currently pursuing Class 11 (Commerce) at Sanjay Ghodawat International School, Aritra is a prominent member of the Student Council, serving as the Deputy Technical CEO. In addition, he plays a pivotal role as the Technical Manager for Bengali Samaj Ichalkaranji, overseeing significant community events such as Durga Puja. Coming from a family with a rich legacy of entrepreneurship, Aritra has inherited a passion for business and innovation. Beyond his academic and leadership pursuits, he oversees marketing and technical strategies for his family's business, Maa Tara Jewellers. His hands-on approach has contributed to the growth and modernization of the fir

Author, Aritra Manna

At just 17, Aritra has already carved out his entrepreneurial path with his firm, Aritra Visual Studio, which has achieved remarkable success, generating ₹35 lakhs in just 1.5 years. This venture reflects his commitment to blending creativity, technology, and strategic thinking to deliver impactful results. In his debut book, "From Dreams to Riches: Inspiring Journeys of Indian Entrepreneurs," Aritra shares the incredible stories of Indian business leaders who have overcome challenges to achieve remarkable success. Through these narratives, he seeks to inspire readers to pursue their dreams with passion and perseverance. Aritra's journey as a young entrepreneur, leader, and storyteller is a testament to his dedication, creativity, and drive to make a difference. With his diverse achievements and unyielding ambition, Aritra is well on his way to leaving a significant mark in the worlds of business and literature.

CHAPTER ONE

THE LANDSCAPE OF ENTREPRENEURSHIP IN INDIA

Introduction

India, often referred to as the "land of opportunities," has evolved into a hub of entrepreneurial energy. Its economy, rich cultural diversity, and vast market potential create an environment ripe for innovation. This chapter explores the growth trajectory of India's economy, the critical role entrepreneurship plays in driving development, the dynamic trends shaping the entrepreneurial ecosystem, and the importance of financial literacy as a cornerstone of success.

The Indian Economy: A Journey of Growth

India's economic journey since independence has been remarkable, transitioning from a primarily agrarian economy to a diversified powerhouse. Today, India is the fifth-largest economy globally, with sectors like technology, manufacturing, and services playing pivotal roles. This rapid growth has unlocked immense opportunities for entrepreneurs, supported by the government's initiatives like Make in India, Digital India, and Startup India. These programs foster innovation, infrastructure development, and ease of doing business.

Entrepreneurship: The Catalyst of Economic Development

Entrepreneurship is the backbone of any thriving economy. In India, it drives job creation, promotes innovation, and elevates living standards. Startups like Flipkart, Zomato, and Ola have not only disrupted traditional industries but also showcased the country's potential on the global stage. Moreover, micro and small enterprises, which constitute over 63 million units, play a vital role in empowering rural areas and promoting inclusive growth. Women entrepreneurs, too, are redefining norms, contributing significantly to sectors ranging from technology to handicrafts.

Trends Shaping the Entrepreneurial Ecosystem

The Indian entrepreneurial ecosystem has undergone a transformation, driven by technological advancements, a burgeoning middle class, and increasing internet penetration. Key trends include:

1. Tech-Driven Startups: AI, blockchain, and IoT are revolutionizing industries such as healthcare, finance, and agriculture.

2. Rise of Social Enterprises: Entrepreneurs are addressing societal challenges like education, sanitation, and renewable energy while maintaining profitability.

3. Funding Boom: Venture capital, angel investors, and crowdfunding platforms have fuelled the growth of innovative startups.

4. Global Aspirations: Indian startups are no longer confined to domestic markets, with many expanding internationally

Financial Literacy:

A Pillar of Entrepreneurial Success Behind every successful entrepreneur lies a sound understanding of finance. Financial literacy—comprehending budgets, investments, and risk management—is crucial for sustainable growth. It equips entrepreneurs to make informed decisions, avoid pitfalls, and optimize resources. 4 In India, initiatives like Pradhan Mantri Jan Dhan Yojana and financial inclusion programs are empowering aspiring entrepreneurs from all backgrounds to gain access to credit, insurance, and investment opportunities. Financial education must start early, encouraging youth to understand the basics of saving, credit, and wealth creation.

India's entrepreneurial landscape is poised for exponential growth. With continued support from government policies, advancements in technology, and the resilience of its people, India is set to become a global leader in innovation. Aspiring entrepreneurs must embrace the spirit of perseverance and innovation while leveraging the vast resources and networks available in today's ecosystem.

CHAPTER TWO

The Mindset of a Millionaire

"Success is not final, failure is not fatal: It is the courage to continue that counts.".

– Winston Churchill

The journey to entrepreneurial success is as much about mindset as it is about strategy. A strong foundation of mental and emotional traits sets successful entrepreneurs apart, enabling them to navigate the tumultuous path of building a business

Characteristics and Traits of Successful Entrepreneurs

1. **Unwavering Confidence:** Confidence doesn't mean knowing all the answers; it's about trusting your ability to figure things out. Entrepreneurs like **Ratan Tata** showcased this during the Nano project, remaining steadfast despite criticism.
2. **Decisiveness:** Successful entrepreneurs make timely decisions, even in uncertainty. **Dhirubhai Ambani,** for instance, consistently made bold moves that disrupted industries
3. **Passion and Drive:** Without a burning passion, sustaining the effort required to grow a business becomes challenging. **Biju Raveendran,** the founder of BYJU'S, turned his love for teaching into India's largest ed-

tech platform

4. **Risk-Taking Ability:** Entrepreneurs embrace calculated risks. **Kiran Mazumdar**-Shaw, India's biotech pioneer, risked her career as a brewmaster to build Biocon, a company that faced societal scepticism but ultimately transformed the healthcare industry.

The Role of Resilience and Adaptability in Business

Building a business is not a straight path; it is a series of peaks and troughs.

1. **Resilience Against Failure:** Failure is often a stepping stone to success. Narayana Murthy, co-founder of Infosys, was rejected by investors and endured financial struggles, yet his resilience laid the foundation for one of India's most respected companies.

1. **Adaptability in Crisis:** During the COVID-19 pandemic, companies that adapted to digital operations survived. **Deepinder Goyal**, the co-founder of Zomato, shifted focus to grocery delivery during the crisis, ensuring business continuity.

Resilient entrepreneurs see opportunities where others see obstacles, adapting to stay relevant

Importance of Vision and Goal-Setting

A powerful vision acts as a guiding star for an entrepreneur, while goals provide the roadmap to achieve it.

1. **Vision as a Motivator:** Vision fuels motivation even when the odds are stacked against you. **Dr. Verghese Kurien**, the father of the White Revolution, envisioned a self-sufficient India in dairy production, leading to the creation of Amul.
2. **Strategic Goal-Setting:** Breaking down the vision into measurable goals ensures progress. **Falguni Nayar**, founder of Nykaa, envisioned an India-first beauty brand. Her goals included capturing the online market, then expanding to physical stores.

3. **Long-Term Perspective:** Entrepreneurs understand that success is a marathon, not a sprint. **Ritesh Agarwal**, founder of OYO, faced criticism for rapid expansion but stayed focused on long-term scalability.

Case Studies: Overcoming Initial Failures

1. **The Story of Flipkart:** Sachin and Binny Bansal started Flipkart as an online bookstore, facing challenges like low customer trust in e-commerce. Their breakthrough came by focusing on customer experience, introducing the concept of cash-on-delivery.
2. **Patanjali: From Struggles to Success:** Acharya Balkrishna and Baba Ramdev initially struggled to establish Patanjali in the FMCG sector, competing with giants like HUL and P&G. Their commitment to authenticity and affordability won over Indian consumers
3. **Vijay Shekhar Sharma's Paytm Journey:** Vijay Sharma faced personal and financial struggles before launching Paytm. His bold pivot from mobile recharge to fintech services during demonetization made Paytm a household name.
4. **The Rise of Ola:** Bhavish Aggarwal faced resistance from drivers and regulatory hurdles in Ola's early days. By building a model that benefitted both drivers and riders, he transformed India's urban commute

Cultivating the Millionaire Mindset
Developing a mindset aligned with success is a continual process:

1. **Learn from Failures:** See each setback as a lesson rather than a roadblock.
2. **Focus on Self-Improvement:** Entrepreneurs like Shiv Nadar continuously invest in learning and personal growth.
3. **Surround Yourself with Positive Influences:** Build a network of mentors, peers, and teams who uplift you
4. **Practice Patience:** Overnight success is a myth; persistence pays off.

CONCLUSION
In conclusion, the mindset of a millionaire is built on a foundation of resilience, adaptability, vision, and a willingness to embrace challenges. These traits, combined with strategic planning, enable entrepreneurs to

overcome hurdles and achieve greatness.

CHAPTER THREE

FINANCIAL LITERACY: THE KEY TO SUCCESS

""Courage is not the absence of fear but the triumph over it."
— Nelson Mandela"

Financial literacy is often overlooked in the entrepreneurial journey, yet it's a crucial component of success. A strong grasp of financial concepts can help entrepreneurs make informed decisions, manage resources effectively, and ultimately achieve their goals.

Understanding Basic Financial Concepts

- **Budgeting:** Creating a budget is essential for tracking income and expenses. It helps entrepreneurs allocate funds for various business needs, such as operational costs, marketing, and employee salaries

- Saving: Setting aside a portion of earnings for future use is a wise financial practice. Entrepreneurs can establish emergency funds to cover unexpected costs or invest in growth opportunities.

- Investing: Investing involves allocating funds to assets with the expectation of generating returns. This can include stocks, bonds, real estate, or business ventures.

The Importance of Financial Planning for Startups

A well-crafted financial plan is a roadmap for a startup's growth. It outlines the company's financial goals, revenue projections, and expense budgets. Key elements of financial planning include:

- **Cash Flow Management**: Monitoring the inflow and outflow of cash is crucial for maintaining liquidity.
- **Profit and Loss Statement**: Tracking revenue and expenses helps assess the business's profitability.
- **Balance Sheet**: Analysing assets, liabilities, and equity provides a snapshot of the company's financial health.

Tools and Resources for Improving Financial Literacy

Numerous tools and resources are available to enhance financial literacy:

- **Financial Literacy Courses**: Online courses and workshops offer structured learning on various financial topics.
- **Financial Advisors**: Consulting with a qualified financial advisor can provide personalized guidance and advice.
- **Financial Software:** Software tools like budgeting apps and accounting software can help manage finances efficiently.
- **Financial Books and Articles**: Reading books and articles on finance can broaden knowledge and inspire financial strategies. Real-Life Examples of Entrepreneurs Who Leveraged Financial Knowledge
- **Ritesh Agarwal (OYO Rooms):** Agarwal's astute financial management and strategic investments fuelled the rapid growth of OYO Rooms.
- **Flipkart Founders**: Sachin Bansal and Binny Bansal's ability to secure funding and optimize financial resources played a pivotal role in Flipkart's success. By prioritizing financial literacy, entrepreneurs can make sound decisions, mitigate risks, and position their businesses for long-term success. Remember, financial knowledge is not just about numbers; it's about empowering yourself to achieve your dreams

Expanding on Financial Literacy: A Deeper Dive

Beyond the Basics While understanding fundamental concepts like budgeting, saving, and investing is essential, financial literacy for entrepreneurs extends far beyond. It involves a comprehensive understanding of financial statements, cash flow management, risk assessment, and strategic financial planning

The Power of Financial Statements

- Income Statement: This statement reveals a company's profitability over a specific period. Entrepreneurs can use it to analyse revenue, expenses, and net income.
- Balance Sheet: A snapshot of a company's financial health at a particular point in time, it showcases assets, liabilities, and equity.
- Cash Flow Statement: This statement tracks the inflow and outflow of cash, providing insights into a company's liquidity.

Mastering Cash Flow Management

Effective cash flow management is crucial for business sustainability. Key strategies include:

- Predictive Cash Flow Forecasting: Anticipating future cash inflows and outflows to make informed decisions.
- Tight Accounts Receivable Management: Ensuring timely payment from customers.
- Strategic Inventory Management: Optimizing inventory levels to avoid excessive costs.
- Negotiating Favourable Payment Terms: Securing favourable payment terms with suppliers.

Risk Assessment and Mitigation

Identifying and mitigating financial risks is a vital aspect of financial literacy. Entrepreneurs should consider:

- **Market Risk:** The potential impact of market fluctuations on revenue and profitability.
- **Credit Risk:** The risk of default on loans or other forms of credit.
- **Operational Risk:** The risk of disruptions to business operations, such as supply chain issues or natural disasters.
- **Financial Risk:** The risk of adverse financial events, such as economic downturns or increased interest rates. Strategic Financial Planning A well-crafted financial plan guides a business toward its long-term goals. Essential components include:
- **Setting Clear Financial Goals:** Defining specific, measurable, achievable, relevant, and time-bound (SMART) financial objectives.
- **Developing a Financial Strategy:** Outlining the steps required to achieve financial goals, including capital acquisition, investment strategies, and risk management.
- **Monitoring and Controlling Finances:** Regularly tracking financial performance and taking corrective action as needed.

Strategic Financial Planning

A well-crafted financial plan guides a business toward its long-term goals. Essential components include:

- **Setting Clear Financial Goals:** Defining specific, measurable, achievable, relevant, and time-bound (SMART) financial objectives.
- **Developing a Financial Strategy:** Outlining the steps required to achieve financial goals, including capital acquisition, investment strategies, and risk management.
- **Monitoring and Controlling Finances:** Regularly tracking financial performance and taking corrective action as needed. Real-World Examples: Lessons from the Masters
- **Dhirubhai Ambani:** Ambani's astute financial acumen, coupled with a keen understanding of market dynamics, propelled Reliance Industries to unprecedented heights.

- **N.R. Narayana Murthy:** As the co-founder of Infosys, Murthy's emphasis on strong financial governance and ethical practices laid the foundation for the company's global success.

Conclusion

Financial literacy is the cornerstone of entrepreneurial success. By mastering financial concepts, managing cash flow effectively, assessing risks, and implementing strategic financial planning, entrepreneurs can navigate the complexities of the business world and achieve their dreams.

CHAPTER FOUR

IDENTIFYING OPPORTUNITIES IN THE MARKET

" "Your network is your net worth."
--Porter Gale "

The journey from a mere dream to a thriving business empire often hinges on the ability to spot opportunities. This chapter delves into the art and science of identifying gaps in the market and capitalizing on them.

Techniques for Market Research and Analysis

Market research is the bedrock of any successful business venture. Here are some key techniques to conduct effective market research:

- **Primary Research:** This involves collecting firsthand data through surveys, interviews, and focus groups. It provides valuable insights into consumer preferences, behaviours, and pain points.
- **Secondary Research:** This entails gathering existing data from various sources like industry reports, government publications, and online databases. It helps in understanding market trends, competitive landscapes, and demographic information.
- **SWOT Analysis:** This framework helps in assessing a business's Strengths, Weaknesses, Opportunities, and Threats. By understanding

these factors, entrepreneurs can identify potential opportunities and mitigate risks.

- **Porter's Five Forces Analysis:** This model analyses the competitive intensity of an industry by examining factors like the threat of new entrants, bargaining power of suppliers and buyers, threat of substitute products, and competitive rivalry.

Recognizing Gaps in the Market and Consumer Needs

A keen eye for gaps in the market is crucial for entrepreneurial success. Here are some strategies to identify these opportunities:

- **Pain Point Analysis:** Identifying problems that consumers face and finding innovative solutions to address them.
- **Trend Spotting:** Staying updated with the latest trends and predicting future consumer needs.
- **Competitive Analysis:** Analysing competitors' strengths and weaknesses to identify areas for differentiation.
- Customer Feedback: Actively seeking feedback from customers to understand their unmet needs and desires.

Case Studies of Successful Businesses That Identified Unique Opportunities

- **Flipkart:** This e-commerce giant identified the need for online shopping in India and capitalized on the growing internet penetration

- **Zomato:** This food delivery platform recognized the increasing demand for convenient food ordering and delivery services.
- **Nykaa:** This beauty and personal care retailer tapped into the growing demand for high-quality beauty products and personalized recommendations.

Strategies for Validating Business Ideas

Once a potential opportunity is identified, it's essential to validate the business idea before investing significant resources. Here are some strategies:

- **Market Testing**: Conducting small-scale tests to gauge customer interest and willingness to pay.
- **Minimum Viable Product (MVP)**: Developing a basic version of the product or service to gather feedback and iterate.
- **Customer Validation Interviews**: Conducting one-on-one interviews with potential customers to understand their needs and preferences.
- **Financial Projections:** Creating realistic financial projections to assess the viability of the business idea. By mastering the art of identifying opportunities and validating business ideas, entrepreneurs can increase their chances of building successful and sustainable businesses.

Identifying Opportunities in the Market

Deeper Dive into Market Research Techniques:

- **Customer Journey Mapping:** Visualizing the customer's experience with a product or service to identify pain points and opportunities for improvement.
- **Competitive Intelligence:** analysing competitors' strategies, strengths, weaknesses, and market positioning to gain a competitive edge.
- **Market Segmentation:** Dividing the market into smaller, more homogeneous groups based on demographics, psychographics, behaviour, or geographic location.
- **Value Proposition Canvas:** A tool to clearly articulate a company's value proposition and customer value proposition. Recognizing Niche Opportunities:
- **Identifying Underserved Markets:** Targeting specific demographics or geographic regions with unique needs and preferences.
- **Leveraging Technology:** Utilizing technology to create innovative products and services that disrupt traditional industries.

- **Sustainability and Ethical Consumption:** Capitalizing on the growing consumer demand for environmentally friendly and socially responsible products

Case Study: A Deeper Dive into Zomato

Zomato's success story is a testament to the power of identifying and capitalizing on market opportunities. By leveraging technology and understanding the evolving food delivery landscape, Zomato

- **Digitalized the Food Industry:** Simplified the process of discovering and ordering food, making it more convenient for consumers.
- **Created a Strong Brand Identity:** Built a strong brand image through innovative marketing campaigns and a user-friendly platform. 16
- **Expanded Beyond Food Delivery:** Diversified into various segments like table reservations, food delivery, and grocery delivery. Validating Business Ideas: Additional Strategies
- **A/B Testing:** Experimenting with different versions of a product or marketing campaign to determine the most effective approach.
- **Prototyping:** Creating physical or digital prototypes to test product functionality and user experience.
- **Crowdfunding:** Leveraging the power of crowdfunding platforms to validate market demand and raise capital.
- **Pilot Programs:** Launching small-scale trials to gather feedback and refine the business model

Conclusion

Identifying and capitalizing on market opportunities is a critical skill for entrepreneurs. By conducting thorough market research, recognizing gaps in the market, and validating business ideas, aspiring entrepreneurs can increase their chances of building successful and sustainable ventures. Additional Tips for Aspiring Entrepreneurs:

- **Embrace a Growth Mindset:** Cultivate a mindset that is open to learning, experimentation, and continuous improvement.
- **Build Strong Relationships:** Network with other entrepreneurs, mentors, and industry experts to gain valuable insights and support.
- **Stay Agile and Adaptable:** Be prepared to pivot your business strategy as market conditions change.
- **Learn from Failures:** View failures as learning opportunities and use them to refine your approach.
- **Never Stop Innovating:** Continuously seek out new ideas and opportunities to stay ahead of the competition.

By following these guidelines and leveraging the techniques discussed in this chapter, aspiring entrepreneurs can embark on their journey towards achieving their dreams of building successful businesses.

Additional Tips for Aspiring Entrepreneurs:

- **Embrace a Growth Mindset:** Cultivate a mindset that is open to learning, experimentation, and continuous improvement.

- **Build Strong Relationships:** Network with other entrepreneurs, mentors, and industry experts to gain valuable insights and support.

- **Stay Agile and Adaptable:** Be prepared to pivot your business strategy as market conditions change.

- **Learn from Failures:** View failures as learning opportunities and use them to refine your approach.

- **Never Stop Innovating**: Continuously seek out new ideas and opportunities to stay ahead of the competition. By following these guidelines and leveraging the techniques discussed in this chapter, aspiring entrepreneurs can embark on their journey towards achieving their dreams of building successful businesses.

- **Never Stop Innovating**: Continuously seek out new ideas and opportunities to stay ahead of the competition. By following these guidelines and leveraging the techniques discussed in this chapter, aspiring entrepreneurs can embark on their journey towards achieving their dreams of building successful businesses.

CHAPTER FIVE

BUILDING A BUSINESS PLAN

""Chase the vision, not the money; the money will end up following you."
— Tony Hsieh **"**

A business plan is the blueprint for your entrepreneurial journey. It outlines your vision, strategies, and financial projections, guiding you towards success. A well-crafted business plan not only helps you secure funding but also serves as a roadmap to navigate the complexities of running a business.

Components of an Effective Business Plan

A comprehensive business plan typically includes the following components:

1. **Executive Summary:** A concise overview of your business idea, target market, financial projections, and funding needs.
2. **Company Description:** A detailed description of your business, its mission, vision, and core values.
3. **Market Analysis:** A thorough analysis of your target market, including market size, trends, competition, and customer segmentation.
4. **Organization and Management:** An outline of your organizational structure, management team, and their qualifications and experience.
5. **Service Line or Product Line:** A detailed description of your products or services, including their unique selling points and competitive advantages.

6. **Marketing and Sales Strategy:** A comprehensive marketing plan outlining your target audience, marketing channels, and sales strategies.
7. **Funding Request:** A clear statement of your funding needs and how the funds will be utilized.
8. **Financial Projections:** Detailed financial projections, including income statements, balance sheets, and cash flow statements.

The Importance of a Clear Value Proposition

A clear value proposition is the heart of your business plan. It articulates the unique value you offer to your customers, differentiating you from competitors. A strong value proposition helps you:

- Attract customers: By clearly communicating the benefits of your product or service.
- Retain customers: By consistently delivering on your value proposition.
- Command premium pricing: By offering a superior value proposition.

Financial Projections and Funding Strategies

Financial projections are essential for assessing the financial viability of your business. They help you:

- **Secure funding:** By demonstrating the potential profitability of your venture.
- **Make informed decisions:** By analysing financial data to identify opportunities and risks.
- **Track performance:** By comparing actual results to projected figures. Funding strategies can vary depending on your business needs and stage of growth. Some common funding options include:
- **Self-funding:** Using personal savings or assets to finance your business.
- **Bootstrapping:** Using minimal resources to start and grow your business.
- **Debt financing:** Borrowing money from banks or other lenders.
- **Equity financing:** Selling ownership shares in your company to investors.
- **Crowdfunding:** Raising funds from a large number of individuals through online platforms

Examples of Successful Business Plans from Indian Entrepreneurs

- **Flipkart:** The e-commerce giant's business plan highlighted the potential of online retail in India, attracting significant investments.
- **Ola:** The ride-hailing company's business plan focused on leveraging technology to disrupt the traditional taxi industry.
- **Zomato:** The food delivery platform's business plan emphasized the growing demand for convenient food delivery services. By carefully crafting a comprehensive business plan, Indian entrepreneurs can increase their chances of success and build thriving business

Crafting a Compelling Business Plan: A Deeper Dive

While the foundational elements of a business plan are crucial, it's the depth and strategic thinking embedded within each section that truly sets apart a successful plan.

Deepening the Market Analysis

- **Customer Segmentation:** Divide your target market into smaller, more defined groups based on demographics, psychographics, or behavioural factors. This granular approach allows you to tailor your marketing and sales strategies to specific segments.
- **Competitive Analysis:** Conduct a detailed analysis of your competitors, including their strengths, weaknesses, market share, and customer base. Identify your unique selling proposition (USP) and how it differentiates you from the competition. 21 Market Trends: Stay updated on industry trends, technological advancements, and regulatory changes that may impact your business. Incorporate these insights into your long-term strategy. Strengthening the Organization and Management Section

- **Team Building:** Outline the roles and responsibilities of key team members, including their qualifications, experience, and contributions to the business.

- **Organizational Structure:** Clearly define the hierarchy and reporting structure within your organization. This ensures efficient decision-making and accountability.

- **Risk Management:** Identify potential risks and develop strategies to mitigate them. This proactive approach can help you navigate challenges and minimize their impact.

Elevating the Marketing and Sales Strategy

- **Marketing Channels:** Determine the most effective marketing channels to reach your target audience, such as social media, content marketing, email marketing, and1 traditional advertising.
- **Sales Process:** Outline your sales process, including lead generation, customer qualification, sales pitch, closing, and post-sales support.
- **Customer Acquisition and Retention:** Develop strategies to attract new customers and retain existing ones through loyalty programs, excellent customer service, and personalized experiences.

Financial Projections: A Closer Look

- **Revenue Forecasting:** Make realistic revenue projections based on market research, sales forecasts, and pricing strategies.
- **Cost Analysis:** Identify and categorize fixed and variable costs, including operational expenses, marketing expenses, and administrative costs.
- **Profit and Loss Statement:** Create a detailed profit and loss statement to project your business's profitability over time. 22
- **Cash Flow Statement:** Analyse your cash inflows and outflows to ensure you have sufficient liquidity to meet your operational needs.
- **Break-Even Analysis:** Calculate the point at which your total revenue equals your total costs, providing valuable insights into your business's financial viability

Funding Strategies and Investor Pitch

- **Investor Presentation:** Prepare a compelling investor presentation that highlights your business's potential, market opportunity, and financial projections.
- **Financial Modelling:** Utilize financial modelling tools to create sophisticated projections and sensitivity analyses.
- **Exit Strategy:** Outline your long-term vision for the business, including potential exit strategies such as acquisition, IPO, or strategic partnership.

Learning from Indian Entrepreneurs

- **Ratan Tata:** Known for his visionary leadership and focus on innovation, Tata's business plans often emphasized long-term sustainability and social impact.
- **Dhirubhai Ambani:** Ambani's aggressive expansion strategies and risk-taking approach were key to the success of Reliance Industries.
- **N.R. Narayana Murthy:** As the co-founder of Infosys, Murthy's emphasis on ethical business practices, quality, and customer satisfaction has been instrumental in the company's growth.

CHAPTER SIX

FUNDING YOUR VENTURE

"Surround yourself with only people who are going to lift you higher."
— Oprah Winfrey

Funding is the lifeblood of any startup. Without adequate financial resources, even the most innovative ideas can wither and die. This chapter delves into the diverse avenues of funding available to Indian entrepreneurs, the art of pitching to investors, and the supportive role of government initiatives

Overview of Funding Options

1. **Bootstrapping**: Self-funding is the most common initial 23 source of capital for startups. It involves using personal savings, revenue generated from the business, and loans from friends and family. While bootstrapping offers complete control, it can limit growth potential.
2. **Loans:** Traditional bank loans and government-backed loans are viable options, especially for established businesses with a strong track record. However, securing loans can be a time-consuming process and often requires collateral.
3. **Venture Capital:** Venture Capital (VC) firms invest in high-growth potential startups in exchange for equity. VCs typically focus on early-stage and growth-stage companies. They bring not only capital but also

valuable industry expertise and networks.

4. **Angel Investors:** Angel investors are wealthy individuals who invest in early-stage companies. They often have a passion for entrepreneurship and are willing to take higher risks for potentially high returns. Angel investors can provide not just capital but also mentorship and guidance.

How to Pitch to Investors Effectively

A compelling pitch is crucial to attract investors. Here are some key tips:

- **Know Your Audience:** Understand the investor's preferences, investment thesis, and portfolio.
- **Tell a Story:** Craft a narrative that highlights the problem your solution solves, the market opportunity, and your team's capabilities.
- **Financial Projections:** Present realistic and conservative financial forecasts.
- **Practice Your Pitch:** Rehearse your pitch multiple times to ensure a smooth delivery.
- **Be Prepared for Questions:** Anticipate questions and have well-thought-out answers

Case Studies of Successful Funding

- **Flipkart:** This e-commerce giant initially bootstrapped its operations. As it scaled, it secured funding from venture capital firms like Accel Partners and Tiger Global Management
- **Zomato:** This food delivery platform raised significant funds from investors like Sequoia Capital India and Info Edge. The Role of Government Schemes and Initiatives the Indian government has launched numerous schemes and initiatives to foster entrepreneurship and provide financial support to startups. Some notable programs include:

- **Startup India:** This initiative offers a range of benefits, including tax breaks, patent filing subsidies, and access to government funding.
- **Mudra Yojana:** This scheme provides loans to micro, small, and medium enterprises. By understanding the diverse funding options, mastering the art of pitching, and leveraging government support, Indian entrepreneurs can fuel their dreams and achieve remarkable success

Expanding Your Chapter: "Funding Your Venture"

To further enrich your chapter, consider delving deeper into these aspects:

1. **Due Diligence and Investor Relations:**

- **Investor Due Diligence:** Explain the rigorous process investors undertake to assess startups, including financial analysis, team evaluation, market research, and legal scrutiny.
- **Building Investor Relationships:** Discuss the importance of networking, attending industry events, and leveraging online platforms to connect with potential investors.
- **Maintaining Investor Relations:** Highlight the significance of regular communication, transparent reporting, and addressing investor concerns promptly

1. **Government Initiatives and Incentives:**

- **State-Level Support:** Explore the various state-specific schemes and incentives, such as tax breaks, subsidies, and grants, offered to startups.
- **International Funding:** Discuss opportunities for Indian startups to raise funds from global venture capital firms and angel investors.
- **Impact Investing:** Highlight the growing trend of impact investing, where investors seek both financial returns and social and environmental impact.

3. **Alternative Funding Sources:**

- **Crowdfunding:** Explain the different types of crowdfunding (equity, reward, donation) and how startups can leverage this platform to raise capital.

- **Debt Financing:** Discuss the pros and cons of debt financing, including term loans, lines of credit, and invoice financing.
- **Corporate Venture Capital:** Explore how large corporations are investing in startups through their corporate venture capital arms. 4. Common Funding Pitfalls and Lessons Learned:
- **Valuation Challenges:** Discuss the complexities of valuing early-stage startups and the importance of realistic valuations.
- **Dilution of Ownership:** Explain how raising capital can lead to dilution of ownership and the strategies to mitigate this.
- **Legal and Tax Implications:** Highlight the legal and tax considerations involved in fundraising, including shareholder agreements, term sheets, and tax implications.

4. **Common Funding Pitfalls and Lessons Learned:**

- **Valuation Challenges:** Discuss the complexities of valuing early-stage startups and the importance of realistic valuations.
- **Dilution of Ownership:** Explain how raising capital can lead to dilution of ownership and the strategies to mitigate this.
- **Legal and Tax Implications:** Highlight the legal and tax considerations involved in fundraising, including shareholder agreements, term sheets, and tax implications

5. **Case Studies: In-Depth Analysis**

- **Detailed Case Studies:** Provide in-depth case studies of Indian startups that have successfully raised significant funding, analysing their strategies, challenges, and lessons learned.
- **Lessons from Failures:** Discuss the reasons behind failed fundraising attempts and the valuable lessons that can be drawn from these experiences. 26 By incorporating these additional elements, you can create a comprehensive and informative chapter that provides aspiring entrepreneurs with a thorough understanding of the funding landscape and equips them with the knowledge and tools to secure the necessary capital for their ventures

CHAPTER SEVEN

Navigating Legal and Regulatory Frameworks

" "Don't sit down and wait for the opportunities to come. Get up and make them."
— Madam C.J. Walker "

Embarking on the entrepreneurial journey in India is an exhilarating experience, but it's essential to navigate the intricate legal and regulatory landscape. Adhering to these frameworks is not just a legal obligation but a strategic imperative for long-term success.

Understanding the Legal Requirements

The specific legal requirements for starting a business in India vary based on the nature and scale of the venture. However, several fundamental steps remain consistent across different business structures:

1. **Choosing the Right Business Structure:**

Proprietorship: A straightforward structure for sole proprietorships, offering simplicity and ease of setup.

- **Partnership**: A partnership between two or more individuals, sharing profits and losses.

- **Private Limited Company:** A popular choice for businesses seeking limited liability, providing a strong corporate structure.

- **Limited Liability Partnership (LLP):** A hybrid structure combining the flexibility of a partnership with the liability protection of a company.

1. Registration and Licensing:

- **Registration:** Registering your business with the Registrar of Companies (ROC) or relevant authorities to establish legal existence.

- **Licenses and Permits:** Obtaining necessary licenses and permits from various government agencies, such as the Food Safety and Standards Authority of India (FSSAI), Goods and Services Tax (GST) authorities, and Pollution Control Boards, depending on the industry and operations.

3. **Tax Registration:**

- **GST Registration**: Registering for GST to comply with tax regulations and collect and remit taxes.
- Income Tax Registration: Obtaining a Permanent Account Number (PAN) for income tax purposes and filing returns.

4. **Labor Laws:**

- Adhering to labor laws, including minimum wages, working hours, social security benefits, and other labor regulations.

5. **Intellectual Property Rights (IPR):**

- Protecting your intellectual property through trademarks, patents, copyrights, and design patents.

The Imperative of Compliance and Ethical Practices

Compliance and ethical practices are not mere legal obligations but the bedrock of a sustainable and reputable business. Non-compliance can lead to severe consequences, including hefty fines, potential imprisonment, and irreparable damage to brand reputation. Key areas of compliance include:

- **Tax Compliance:** Timely filing of tax returns and payment of taxes to avoid penalties and interest.
- **Labor Law Compliance:** Adhering to labour laws, ensuring fair labour practices, and providing a safe and healthy work environment.
- **Environmental Compliance:** Complying with environmental regulations, minimizing environmental impact, and promoting sustainable practices.
- **Consumer Protection:** Adhering to consumer protection laws, ensuring fair business practices, and prioritizing customer satisfaction.
- **Corporate Social Responsibility (CSR):** Engaging in CSR activities to give back to society, enhance brand reputation, and contribute to sustainable development.

Overcoming Legal Challenges: Case Studies

Numerous successful Indian entrepreneurs have encountered legal challenges during their entrepreneurial journeys. Here are a few inspiring case studies:

- **Case Study 1: The Food Startup** A food startup faced significant hurdles related to FSSAI licensing and stringent food safety regulations. By hiring experienced legal counsel and investing in rigorous quality control measures, they successfully navigated these challenges and built a thriving brand.

- **Case Study 2: The E-commerce Venture** An e-commerce venture encountered complexities with customs duties and import regulations. Through meticulous research, consultation with customs brokers, and strategic planning, they streamlined their import processes and minimized costs

Resources for Legal Assistance and Guidance

To effectively navigate the intricate legal landscape, entrepreneurs can leverage the following resources:

- **Legal Professionals:** Consult with experienced lawyers specializing in corporate law, tax law, and intellectual property law to receive tailored advice.

- **Chartered Accountants:** Seek guidance from chartered accountants for tax and financial compliance.
- **Government Websites:** Utilize government websites to access relevant laws, regulations, notifications, and guidelines.
- **Business Associations:** Join business associations to network with fellow entrepreneurs, share experiences, and gain valuable insights.
- **Legal Aid Clinics:** Seek affordable legal assistance from government-sponsored legal aid clinics. By understanding the legal requirements, prioritizing compliance, and seeking expert advice, Indian entrepreneurs can build successful and sustainable businesses that contribute to the nation's economic growth.

CHAPTER EIGHT

MARKETING STRATEGIES FOR GROWTH

""A brand is no longer what we tell the consumer it is—it is what consumers tell each other it is."
— Scott Coo"

In today's dynamic business landscape, effective marketing is the cornerstone of sustainable growth. It's the art and science of connecting with your target audience, understanding their needs, and persuading them to choose your products or services. Whether you're a budding entrepreneur or a seasoned business leader, a well-crafted marketing strategy can significantly influence the trajectory of your business.

Traditional Marketing Techniques: A Timeless Approach

While the digital age has revolutionized marketing, traditional methods still hold significant value. These techniques, often referred to as offline marketing, can complement your digital efforts and help you reach a broader audience.

- **Print Media:** Newspapers, magazines, and brochures can be highly effective for reaching niche markets and building brand credibility.
- **Television and Radio Advertising:** These channels offer unparalleled reach, allowing you to broadcast your message to a vast audience.
- **Outdoor Advertising:** Billboards, hoardings, and transit advertising can create a strong visual impact and increase brand visibility.
- **Public Relations:** Cultivating relationships with media outlets can generate positive publicity and enhance brand reputation.

Digital Marketing: Navigating the Online World

Digital marketing has transformed the way businesses interact with customers. By leveraging online platforms, you can target specific demographics, measure the impact of your campaigns, and optimize your marketing efforts in real-time.

- Search Engine Optimization (SEO): Improving your website's visibility on search engines like Google can drive organic traffic and attract potential customers.
- Pay-Per-Click (PPC) Advertising: Running targeted ads on search engines and social media platforms can help you reach your audience quickly and effectively.
- Social Media Marketing: Engaging with your audience on platforms like Facebook, Instagram, Twitter, and LinkedIn can foster brand loyalty, drive sales, and generate valuable customer insights.
- Content Marketing: Creating high-quality content, such as blog posts, articles, and videos, can attract and retain customers, establish thought leadership, and improve your website's search engine rankings.
- Email Marketing: Building and nurturing an email list can help you stay connected with your customers, promote your products or services, and drive repeat business

The Power of Branding and Customer Engagement

A strong brand identity is the foundation of successful marketing. Your brand should reflect your values, mission, and unique selling proposition. Consistent branding across all marketing channels can help you differentiate yourself from competitors and create a lasting impression on your audience. Customer engagement is equally important. By actively listening to your customers, responding to their feedback, and providing exceptional customer service, you can build trust, loyalty, and advocacy.

Case Studies of Successful Marketing Campaigns in India

- *Flipkart's **The Big Billion Days**: This annual sale event has become a cultural phenomenon, leveraging digital marketing, social media, and strategic partnerships to drive massive sales and brand awareness.*
- ***Swiggy's Innovative Marketing Campaigns:** Swiggy has consistently used humor, nostalgia, and timely marketing campaigns to connect with its target audience, increase brand recall, and drive app downloads*

Tips for Leveraging Social Media and Online Platforms

• Define Your Target Audience: Identify your ideal customer and tailor your content to their preferences and interests.

• Create High-Quality Content: Develop content that is informative, engaging, and visually appealing.

• Utilize Visual Content: Incorporate images, videos, and infographics to enhance your content's impact.

• Engage with Your Audience: Respond to comments, messages, and reviews promptly and professionally.

• Run Contests and Giveaways: Encourage user-generated content, foster community, and generate excitement.

• Track Your Performance: Use analytics tools to measure the effectiveness of your campaigns and make data-driven decisions. By combining traditional and digital marketing techniques, and focusing on branding and customer engagement, you can create a powerful marketing strategy that drives growth, enhances brand reputation, and ultimately leads to sustained success

CHAPTER NINE

TECHNOLOGY AS A CATALYST FOR SUCCESS

""Change is the heartbeat of growth."
— Scottie Somers "

Technology has irrevocably transformed the entrepreneurial landscape, offering unprecedented opportunities for innovation and growth. Indian entrepreneurs have been at the forefront of this technological revolution, leveraging digital tools to disrupt industries, create new markets, and redefine business models

The Digital Revolution and Entrepreneurship

The advent of the digital age has democratized entrepreneurship, lowering barriers to entry and empowering individuals to turn their ideas into reality. By leveraging technology, entrepreneurs can:

● **Optimize Operations:** Implement automation and AI-powered tools to streamline processes, reduce costs, and enhance efficiency.

● **Expand Market Reach:** Utilize e-commerce platforms, social media, and digital marketing to connect with a global audience and scale their businesses.

● **Personalize Customer Experiences:** Leverage data analytics to gain insights into customer behaviour, preferences, and needs, enabling tailored marketing strategies and improved customer satisfaction.

• **Foster Innovation:** Embrace emerging technologies like artificial intelligence, machine learning, and blockchain to develop innovative products and services.

Indian Tech Titans: A Testament to Innovation

India has produced a plethora of successful tech startups that have made a significant impact on the global stage. Some notable examples include:

• **Flipkart:** This e-commerce giant revolutionized online shopping in India, challenging traditional retail models and setting new industry standards.

• **Paytm:** By simplifying digital payments and offering a wide range of financial services, Paytm has empowered millions of Indians to embrace the digital economy.

• **Ola and Uber:** These ride-hailing companies have transformed urban mobility, providing convenient and affordable transportation solutions.

• **Zomato and Swiggy:** These food delivery platforms have disrupted the food industry, connecting customers with a diverse range of restaurants.

The Future of Tech-Driven Entrepreneurship

As technology continues to evolve, the opportunities for Indian entrepreneurs are boundless. To stay ahead of the curve, entrepreneurs should:

• Embrace Continuous Learning: Stay updated with the latest technological advancements and industry trends.

• Foster a Culture of Innovation: Encourage creativity, experimentation, and risk-taking within their organizations.

• Build Strong Technology Teams: Recruit and retain talented tech professionals to drive innovation.

• Collaborate with Tech Partners: Partner with technology companies, accelerators, and incubators to access resources and expertise.

• Prioritize Cybersecurity: Implement robust cybersecurity measures to protect sensitive data and mitigate risks. By leveraging technology and embracing innovation, Indian entrepreneurs can continue to shape the future of the Indian economy and make a significant global impact

CHAPTER TEN

BUILDING A STRONG TEAM: THE FOUNDATION OF ENTREPRENEURIAL SUCCESS

"Great things in business are never done by one person; they're done by a team of people."
— Steve Jobs

A successful business is not merely a brilliant idea or a well-crafted strategy; it's the people who bring it to life. A strong team is the backbone of any organization, and building one is a critical skill for every entrepreneur.

The Art of Hiring: Finding the Right Fit

The first step towards building a strong team is to hire the right people. While technical skills and experience are important, it's equally crucial to assess a candidate's cultural fit and alignment with the company's values. Here are some key qualities to look for in potential team members:

• **Passion and Drive**: A genuine enthusiasm for the company's mission and a strong work ethic.

- **Adaptability and Resilience:** The ability to embrace change, learn quickly, and overcome challenges.
- **Teamwork and Collaboration:** A willingness to work collaboratively with others and contribute to a positive team culture.
- **Problem-Solving Skills:** The ability to think critically, analyse problems, and develop innovative solutions.
- **Effective Communication:** Strong written and verbal communication skills to convey ideas clearly and concisely.
- **Emotional Intelligence:** The ability to understand and manage emotions, both their own and those of others.
- **Continuous Learning Mindset:** A commitment to lifelong learning and professional development.

Cultivating a High-Performance Culture

Once you've assembled a talented team, it's essential to create a positive and supportive work environment that fosters growth and innovation. Key strategies for building a high-performance culture
include:

- **Clear Communication:** Open and honest communication is essential for building trust and alignment within the team.
- **Empowerment:** Empowering team members to take ownership of their work and make decisions can boost morale and productivity.
- **Recognition and Rewards:** Recognizing and rewarding employees for their achievements can motivate and inspire them.
- **Continuous Learning and Development:** Investing in employee training and development can help them stay updated with the latest trends and improve their skills.
- **Work-Life Balance:** Promoting a healthy work-life balance can enhance employee satisfaction and retention.
- **Strong Leadership:** Effective leadership is crucial for guiding the team, setting clear expectations, and providing support.
- **Mentorship and Coaching:** Providing mentorship and coaching opportunities can help team members develop their skills and advance their careers.

- **Celebrating Successes:** Recognizing and celebrating team and individual achievements can boost morale and create a positive work environment.
- **Encouraging Feedback:** Creating a culture where feedback is valued and used to improve performance can help individuals and teams grow.

Case Studies in Team Building

Many successful Indian entrepreneurs have built strong teams that have been instrumental in their success. For example:

- **Infosys:** Narayana Murthy's vision and leadership, combined with the dedication and hard work of his team, transformed Infosys into a global IT giant.
- **Flipkart:** Sachin Bansal and Binny Bansal built a strong team that helped Flipkart disrupt the Indian e-commerce market.
- **Zomato:** Deepinder Goyal and Pankaj Chandah built a passionate team that transformed the way people order food in India. By investing in your team, fostering a positive culture, and providing opportunities for growth and development, you can build a strong foundation for long-term success

CHAPTER ELEVEN

THE DNA OF A SUCCESSFUL ENTREPRENEUR

In India, entrepreneurship isn't just about starting a business; it's a journey filled with challenges, risks, and triumphs. The entrepreneurial landscape has witnessed a transformation, with individuals from diverse backgrounds making their mark. But what sets successful entrepreneurs apart from the rest? Is it just luck, or is there a pattern—a DNA—that defines them? In this chapter, we dive deep into the characteristics, mindset, and strategies that shape a successful entrepreneur in India.

11.1 The Mindset of an Entrepreneur

The first and foremost thing that differentiates an entrepreneur from a regular businessperson is the mindset. Entrepreneurship isn't just about making money; it's about solving problems, creating value, and making an impact.

11.1.1 Risk-taking vs. Calculated Risks

One of the biggest myths about entrepreneurship is that successful businesspeople are extreme risk-takers. While risk is inevitable, great entrepreneurs don't gamble blindly. They take **calculated risks**, assessing the potential gains and losses before making a move.

Take the example of **Ritesh Agarwal, the founder of OYO Rooms**. When he started his journey, the hotel industry was dominated by large chains, and no one thought an aggregator model would work. But Ritesh saw an opportunity—millions of budget traveller's in India who wanted clean, affordable stays. Instead of investing in his own hotels (which would have been highly risky), he built a network of budget hotels under a single brand, using technology and a standardized service model. The calculated risk paid off, making OYO a billion-dollar company.

11.2 The Power of Persistence and Resilience

Entrepreneurs fail more times than they succeed. But the key difference is **how they handle failure**. Every successful business leader has faced setbacks, but they persist despite challenges.

11.2.1 The Story of Dhirubhai Ambani

Dhirubhai Ambani, the founder of Reliance, started with nothing. He worked in a gas station in Yemen before returning to India with a dream of building an empire. When he started Reliance, he faced skepticism from established business houses, legal battles, and financial roadblocks. But he persisted, focusing on innovation and affordable pricing, which eventually led Reliance to become India's largest business conglomerate.

11.2.2 Failure as a Learning Experience

- **Sachin Bansal and Binny Bansal (Flipkart founders)** initially faced multiple rejections when seeking funding. But they kept tweaking their model, shifting from a simple online bookstore to an e-commerce giant.
- **Kunal Shah (CRED founder)** failed with his first startup, FreeCharge, but used those lessons to build a more successful fintech company later.

The key lesson? **Failure isn't the opposite of success—it's a stepping stone towards it.**

11.3 The Role of Passion and Vision

Successful entrepreneurs aren't just in business to make money. They are driven by **passion** and a **vision** bigger than themselves.

- **Steve Jobs (Apple)** was obsessed with design and user experience.
- **Elon Musk (Tesla, SpaceX)** has a vision of making humanity multi-planetary.
- **Narayan Murthy (Infosys)** wanted to put India on the global IT map.

11.3.1 Why Passion Matters

Passion gives entrepreneurs the **fuel to keep going**, even during tough times. Many business owners lose motivation when things get difficult, but passionate entrepreneurs keep pushing forward.

Example: **Byju Raveendran (Byju's founder)** started as a teacher who wanted to make learning engaging. His passion for education led to the creation of one of India's largest EdTech platforms, revolutionizing online learning.

11.4 Adaptability: The Key to Long-Term Success

The business world is constantly changing. The best entrepreneurs are **adaptable**—they pivot when necessary and embrace change.

11.4.1 The Pandemic Lesson

The COVID-19 pandemic showed us how businesses that adapted survived, while others collapsed. Restaurants that shifted to cloud kitchens, offline businesses that moved online, and companies that embraced remote work thrived.

- **Zomato quickly pivoted from food delivery to grocery delivery during the pandemic, keeping its business alive.**

- **Reliance Jio adapted to the digital wave, expanding beyond telecom into e-commerce and payments.**

Adaptability isn't just about **survival**—it's about thriving in a rapidly evolving world.

11.5 Case Studies of Indian Entrepreneurs Who Embody This DNA

11.5.1 Falguni Nayar (Nykaa Founder)

Falguni Nayar was a former investment banker who took the bold step of starting an online beauty and wellness platform at a time when e-commerce in India was still growing. **Her vision, persistence, and adaptability made Nykaa a billion-dollar brand** and a pioneer in the beauty industry.

11.5.2 Kiran Mazumdar-Shaw (Biocon Founder)

Kiran Mazumdar-Shaw started Biocon in a small garage, facing immense challenges as a woman entrepreneur in the biotech sector. Her **resilience and passion** helped Biocon become one of India's leading pharmaceutical companies

Conclusion: The Entrepreneur's DNA in Action

The journey of an entrepreneur isn't easy, but those who succeed have:

- A **calculated risk-taking approach**
- **Persistence and resilience** in the face of failure
- **Passion and vision** that drive them forward
- **Adaptability** to navigate changing markets

Every aspiring entrepreneur in India can learn from these traits and apply them to their journey. Whether you're starting a business in tech, retail, or finance, understanding the **DNA of success** is the first step towards building something truly great.

CHAPTER TWELVE

THE SUCCESS STORY OF MAA TARA JEWELLERS

A Journey of Resilience and Innovation

"Dreams become reality when passion meets perseverance. Maa Tara is not just a brand; it's a legacy built on unwavering dedication and trust."
— Vishwajit Manna

Maa Tara Jewellers (MTJ) is not just a business; it's a legacy built on passion, hard work, and a vision to redefine the jewellery industry.

12.1 OWNER OF MTJ

Founded in 2001 by my father, Vishwajit Manna, and my uncle Prasenjit Manna, MTJ's journey is a testament to the power of resilience and unwavering determination. But the roots of this success story stretch even further back to Maa Tara Works (MTW), a sub-brand established before MTJ, which played a key role in setting the foundation for the jewellery empire that exists today.

Maa Tara Works, with its three workshops across India, has been a crucial pillar in our success. These workshops focus on the highest standards of craftsmanship, providing both MTJ and MTW with unmatched expertise in jewellery manufacturing. The dedication to quality at every step has been vital in building our brand's reputation for excellence.

In 2014, MTJ was born out of my father's vision to create a jewellery brand that combines traditional craftsmanship with modern design and innovative approaches. His belief was simple yet powerful: to provide customers not just with beautiful jewellery but with an experience rooted in trust, quality, and attention to detail. Alongside him, my uncle, Prasenjit Manna, a partner in both MTW and MTJ, played an instrumental role in overseeing daily operations, ensuring that each piece of jewellery met our rigorous standards.

12.2 LOGO OF MTJ

For me, growing up in this environment meant learning firsthand from my father and uncle the values of hard work, dedication, and innovation. From an early age, I saw how they built the business, overcoming challenges and transforming every obstacle into an opportunity. As a

12.3 CO-OWNER OF MTJ

member of the next generation, I have taken on the responsibility of overseeing the marketing and technical aspects of the firm, ensuring that the legacy they built continues to evolve with modern trends and technologies. One of the most inspiring parts of this journey has been witnessing how my father and uncle navigated the competitive jewellery industry with a clear vision and a deep commitment to their craft. Their partnership, grounded in mutual respect and a shared mission, has been the driving force behind our success. What makes MTJ stand out is not just our stunning jewellery, but the relationships we've built with our customers over the years. The personalized service and our focus on quality have helped MTJ become a trusted name in the industry. Today,

Maa Tara Jewellers stands tall as a symbol of quality, craftsmanship, and innovation.

But this success is not just about business growth—it's about the lessons we've learned, the challenges we've overcome, and the impact we continue to make. As I step into the future, continuing the work my father and uncle began, I am inspired by the foundation they've laid. Their vision for the company, combined with my dedication to advancing it, ensures that MTJ will continue to grow and inspire future generations of entrepreneurs. The success of Maa Tara Jewellers is a journey that reflects the power of family, innovation, and determination. It shows that with hard work, vision, and a relentless pursuit of excellence, any dream can be transformed into a lasting legacy. This story is not just about business success; it's about the power of perseverance, passion, and the belief that no challenge is too great when you are committed to your vision.

CHAPTER THIRTEEN

YouTubers as Entrepreneurs

In recent years, India has witnessed a digital revolution, and YouTube has become a powerful platform for content creators to transform their passion into businesses. Indian YouTubers have not only gained immense popularity for their videos but have also established successful brands that cater to millions of fans. This chapter explores how YouTubers in India have evolved from content creators to entrepreneurs, using their platforms to launch diverse business ventures. One notable example of this evolution is **Tech Burner** (Shivam Agrawal) and **Flying Beast** (Gaurav Taneja), whose journeys demonstrate how YouTubers can build empires with a strategic blend of entertainment, technology, and lifestyle.

Case Study 1: Flying Beast – From Vlogs to Fitness and Merchandise

Gaurav Taneja, the creator behind *Flying Beast*, started as a vlogger documenting his daily life, travels, and fitness routines. Over time, his engaging vlogs and inspirational fitness content gained him a huge following. Gaurav's authenticity, combined with his relatable approach to fitness and family life, made him a favourite among his audience. As his brand grew, Gaurav expanded into fitness merchandise, training programs, and collaborations with brands in the fitness industry.

Brand Layers:

- **Entertainment and Vlogging:** Gaurav's vlogs capture his everyday life, from family moments to travel and adventures, making his content relatable and highly engaging for his audience.

- **Fitness and Wellness:** A fitness enthusiast, Gaurav built his fitness brand through workout tips, meal plans, and motivational content, encouraging his fans to lead healthier lives.
- **Merchandise and Collaborations:** Flying Beast's merchandise, including fitness-related products, apparel, and accessories, caters to his audience's lifestyle choices. Gaurav also collaborated with health and fitness brands to expand his reach in the industry.

Case Study 2: Prajakta Koli (Mostly Sane) – From Comedy to Advocacy and Fashion

Prajakta Koli, known for her channel *Mostly Sane*, has built a brand based on relatability, humor, and advocacy. As one of the leading female creators in India, Prajakta has not only entertained her audience with lifestyle content but has also used her platform to raise awareness about important social issues. Her entrepreneurial journey expanded into fashion with her own line of merchandise and collaborations with international brands.

Brand Layers:

- **Relatable Content:** Prajakta's content focuses on everyday topics like relationships, societal expectations, and personal growth, making her relatable to young Indian women.
- **Social Advocacy:** She has been an advocate for important causes, such as mental health and gender equality, strengthening her bond with a socially conscious audience.
- **Merchandise and Fashion:** Prajakta has launched her own line of merchandise, collaborating with well-known brands, offering a diverse range of products that reflect her unique style.

Case Study 3: Tech Burner – Building a Digital Empire with Tech Content

Shivam Agrawal, the mind behind *Tech Burner*, is a perfect example of how a tech YouTuber can build a thriving brand around product reviews, tech tips, and gadget unboxings. Known for his engaging style and relatable content, Tech Burner not only shares tech insights but also educates his audience on the latest gadgets, innovations, and tech trends. What sets him apart is his ability to create a personal connection with his audience while simultaneously positioning himself as an authority in the tech space.

Shivam's brand has grown into a diverse set of ventures through his firm **Brand Overlays and Layers**, which manages his brand extensions and business operations. These include collaborations with major tech companies, launching his own merchandise, and offering digital marketing services.

Brand Layers:

- **Tech Content Creation:** The core of Tech Burner's brand is his tech-related videos, focusing on in-depth reviews, tips, and unboxings of the latest gadgets and tech news.
- **Merchandise and Lifestyle Products:** Shivam has expanded his brand by introducing merchandise like T-shirts, caps, and accessories, which resonate with his audience and extend his personal brand into the consumer space.
- **Business Ventures:** Through **Brand Overlays and Layers**, Tech Burner has ventured into the digital marketing and tech consulting arena, offering services to tech brands looking to expand their reach.

Brand Overlays and Layers: The Power of Tech Burner's Strategic Approach

Tech Burner's **Brand Overlays and Layers** is a business model that extends his core tech content into several business areas. The model shows how YouTubers can build diverse revenue streams by integrating brand extensions that complement their original content.

1. **Tech as the Foundation:** Tech Burner started with content that appeals to a tech-savvy audience, offering honest, accessible reviews and tech tips.
2. **Product Launches and Merchandise:** He created his own line of merchandise and tech products, capitalizing on his audience's trust and loyalty. These products are not just about branding but resonate with his fans' lifestyle choices.
3. **Business Ventures in Digital Marketing:** Through **Brand Overlays and Layers**, Tech Burner expanded his reach by offering digital marketing

strategies and consulting to other tech companies. His understanding of social media and tech trends has given him an edge in providing these services to a wide array of brands.

4. **Engaging and Interactive Community**: Shivam has maintained strong engagement with his fans, frequently interacting with them through social media, YouTube comments, and live events. His audience's feedback has been instrumental in shaping his products and services, ensuring that they remain aligned with what the fans want.

Conclusion: The Future of YouTube Entrepreneurship in India

India's YouTube landscape has transformed from a space for entertainment to an ecosystem where creators can establish successful brands. By blending creativity, authenticity, and entrepreneurial spirit, Indian YouTubers have turned digital platforms into dynamic businesses that continue to grow.

For aspiring entrepreneurs, these YouTubers offer a blueprint on how to leverage digital platforms to build brands that can impact millions. Their journeys prove that with creativity, hard work, and an engaged audience, anything is possible in the digital age. Whether you're looking to entertain, educate, or inspire, YouTube provides a unique space for creating a brand that speaks to the heart of the Indian consumer. Tech Burner's **Brand Overlays and Layers** and Flying Beast's expansion into fitness and merchandise serve as prime examples of how YouTubers can seamlessly extend their digital success into tangible, profitable business ventures.

CHAPTER FOURTEEN

BUILT BY GRIT: THE RISE OF MADAN KARANDE AND THE BALAJI LEGACY

1. Humble Beginnings: Seeds of a Dream

In the small agricultural heartlands of Maharashtra, young Madan Karande spent his early days tending to fields under the sun. Life was simple, but far from easy. Farming taught him discipline, perseverance, and a profound respect for hard work — lessons that would later become the bedrock of his monumental success.

Despite limited resources, Madan Sir dared to dream bigger. He believed that destiny is not inherited; it is built — with vision, determination, and relentless action. In a world where many accepted their circumstances, he chose to challenge them.

> *"I had no roadmap, no blueprint. Just a dream to create something larger than myself — and the belief that hard work could shape the impossible into reality."*
> *— Madan Karande"*

2. The First Brick: Building Balaji Pat Sanstha

In the early days, when financial services were a distant dream for common people in smaller towns, Madan Karande stepped forward to bridge this gap. His first major entrepreneurial leap came with the founding of Balaji Pat Sanstha, a financial cooperative designed to provide affordable credit and financial inclusion to the underserved.

Balaji Pat Sanstha wasn't just a business; it was a movement — offering hope to farmers, small business owners, and families seeking economic freedom.

Through Balaji Pat Sanstha, thousands found a path to empowerment, and Madan Sir laid the cornerstone of what would soon become a growing empire rooted in service, trust, and community development.

3. Sweet Success: The Story of Balaji Bakers

Parallel to these new ventures, the family's original love for bringing smiles to people's faces continues through Balaji Bakers — established in 1995. Over the years, the bakery has become a household name for delicious cakes, fresh breads, and mouth-watering pastries.

With a focus on quality, customer satisfaction, and innovation, Balaji Bakers has mastered the art of turning simple ingredients into moments of joy.

Today, Balaji Bakers is not just a bakery; it's a brand built on trust, taste, and the traditions of excellence.

The logo of Balaji Bakers Ichalkaranji

4. Enlightening Generations: The Birth of Balaji Group of Institutes

Realizing that true transformation comes from education, Madan Sir turned his focus toward another pillar of societal growth — learning.

With a vision to nurture young minds, he established the Balaji Group of Institutes, which today boasts 10 schools and colleges under its umbrella. These institutions serve as centers of academic excellence, empowering students not just with knowledge, but with values and confidence to lead in tomorrow's world.

> *"Buildings can crumble. Businesses can fail. But the power of an educated mind can rebuild a nation."*
> *— Madan Karande*

Today, the Balaji Group of Institutes stands as a beacon of hope for thousands of families across Maharashtra, ensuring that no dream remains unrealized for lack of opportunity.

5. A Voice for the People: Madan Karande's Political Journey

For Madan Karande, entrepreneurship was never just about profits — it was about impact. His growing influence and sincere commitment to public service naturally led him into the world of politics.

Active in local governance, Madan Karande quickly became a respected leader known for his grassroots connect and his unwavering commitment to his people. Though he contested from the opposition party, he garnered major votes and widespread respect, a true testament to his leadership and the trust he commanded among the masses.

> *"Positions come and go. True leadership is about standing by your people — in victory, in defeat, always."*
> *— Madan Karande*

Madan Karande

Even today, he continues to serve as a guiding force in his community, using his influence to drive positive change.

6. The Next Chapter: Balaji Karande and the Spirit of Innovation

The legacy that Madan Karande built is not just one of institutions and businesses; it is a living spirit passed on to the next generation — especially to his son, Balaji Karande.

Growing up amidst entrepreneurship and service, Balaji inherited not just his father's name, but his ambition, work ethic, and passion to innovate. With fresh ideas and a modern approach, he ventured into new avenues, paving his own path while upholding the values his father instilled in him.

Balaji Karande

7. Mini Highlight: B Cafe — Brewing Dreams

One of Balaji Karande's proud ventures is B Cafe, a stylish, modern café born from his passion for bringing people together over great coffee and cozy vibes.

B Cafe is not just a coffee shop; it's a youthful, vibrant space that has quickly become a favorite hangout spot in Ichalkaranji. Offering a curated menu of premium coffee, quick bites, and desserts, it represents a perfect blend of tradition and innovation — the old-world charm of hard work, served with a contemporary twist.

Logo of B cafe

"B Cafe is my dream brewed into reality — a place where stories are shared, ideas are born, and every sip tastes like ambition."
— Balaji Karande

Through B Cafe, Balaji has proven that the entrepreneurial flame in the Karande family burns brighter than ever, adapting to new times without losing the essence of their roots.

8. A Legacy Carved in Hard Work

What makes the Karande story so extraordinary is not fortune, but pure, tireless hard work.

Every business, every institution, every initiative — all are the result of years of effort, sacrifice, sleepless nights, and relentless perseverance. Madan Karande and his family have shown that true success does not come overnight; it is earned — one small step at a time, over years of dedication.

Their journey from humble fields to multifaceted businesses and institutions is a shining example for all entrepreneurs that no matter where you start, your dreams can touch the sky — if you have the courage to work for them.

9. *Final Words: A Tribute to Grit and Greatness*

Madan Karande's life is a celebration of what one can achieve with unwavering determination. It's a legacy that now finds fresh energy through his son Balaji, ensuring that the flame of dreams continues to burn bright for generations to come.

Their story isn't just about business.
It's about belief.
It's about building.
It's about becoming.

From the first plow in the fields to the buzzing halls of schools, from cooperative banks to cozy cafes, from small beginnings to massive impact — the Karande legacy stands as living proof:
Hard work never goes unrewarded.

10. *Balaji and Madan Karande: Influencers of the New Era*

Today, both Madan Karande and Balaji Karande have also made their mark on social media:

Balaji Karande (@balajikarande24): 182 posts, 10.1K followers, inspiring youth through his entrepreneurial journey and vibrant initiatives.

Madan Karande (@madankarande): 1,686 posts, 12.7K followers, with just 38 following — showing his strong connect with people. His profile proudly states: "प्रातंकि सदस्य, राष्ट्रवादी काँग्रेस पार्टी - शरदचंद्र पवार."

Their strong presence reflects their growing influence, not just offline but online too, making them modern torchbearers of leadership, innovation, and community spirit.

Their story teaches us a vital lesson — in a world chasing shortcuts, real influence comes not from instant fame, but from years of dedication, resilience, and a genuine desire to uplift others.
Through hard work, vision, and heart, Balaji and Madan Karande are proving that it's possible to be both entrepreneurs and changemakers — shaping not just businesses, but entire communities and futures.

Author's Note

Writing about the journey of Madan Karande Sir and Balaji Karande feels incredibly personal to me.

I've had the privilege of knowing Balaji not just as a brilliant entrepreneur, but as a lifelong friend, someone whose dedication, humility, and energy constantly inspire me.

Through this chapter, I wanted to celebrate not just their achievements, but the values they stand for — grit, vision, and community spirit.

The Karande family's story reminds us that greatness is not born — it is built, one day, one dream, and one daring step at a time.

Their journey fuels my own dreams, and I hope it fuels yours too.

— Aritra Manna

OLD MUMBAI ICE CREAMS

– A Legacy of Resilience and Sweet Success

"Success is not final, failure is not fatal: it is the courage to continue that counts."
— Winston Churchill

The journey of **Old Mumbai Ice Creams** is not just a business tale; it's a testament to the power of dreams, perseverance, and the ability to adapt. From a humble hawker selling malva and gland ice creams on the streets of Ichalkaranji to a brand with **franchises across India and Dubai**, this story is one of grit and glory.

The Origins: Where It All Began

In the early 1980s, **Mr. Rambabu Ramraj Sharma**, a man with indomitable courage, arrived in Ichalkaranji after struggling to find his footing in Belgaum and Mumbai. With no formal training but a burning desire to make a difference, he began selling ice creams. His product, though simple, carried a unique flavour inspired by the street-side kulfis and treats he encountered in Mumbai.

Armed with a cart and an unwavering spirit, he worked tirelessly under the scorching sun, often barefoot. What started as a ₹5-a-day cart grew steadily as people began relishing his creations. It wasn't just ice cream; it was a symbol of hard work and dedication.

The Transformation: From Cart to Brand

By 1998, Mr. Sharma transitioned from a street vendor to a shop owner, marking the beginning of a significant transformation. His ability to adapt to changing market trends while staying rooted in tradition became the cornerstone of his success.

The turning point came in 2015, when the brand underwent a modern rebranding. With aesthetically designed parlours, innovative Flavors, and a structured business model, Old Mumbai Ice Creams began its journey as a national and international brand. Franchising became a key growth strategy, with outlets now operating in **over 25 locations, including Dubai**. The brand diversified further in 2017 with *Old Mumbai Foods*, offering healthy products like honey, flax seeds, and amla.

Lessons from the Journey

The story of Old Mumbai Ice Creams offers valuable lessons for entrepreneurs and dreamers alike:

1. **Start Small, Dream Big:** Mr. Sharma's journey from a ₹5 cart to a multi-crore empire shows that success begins with taking the first step, no matter how small.
2. **Adapt and Innovate:** The brand's evolution from traditional kulfi carts to modern parlours with unique offerings highlights the importance of staying relevant in a competitive market.
3. **Hard Work Pays Off:** Mr. Sharma's relentless effort, despite sleeping on footpaths and facing countless rejections, underscores the value of perseverance.
4. **Embrace Collaboration:** Partnerships, like the one with Mr. Uday Waldemar, played a crucial role in expanding the brand's reach. Collaboration amplifies growth and brings fresh perspectives.
5. **Diversity is Strength:** By diversifying into health-focused products with *Old Mumbai Foods*, the brand ensured sustainability and expanded its customer base.

Conclusion: More Than Just Ice Cream

Old Mumbai Ice Creams is not merely a business; it's a symbol of resilience and transformation. It reflects how vision, hard work, and adaptability can overcome even the toughest challenges.

For Mr. Sharma, success was not just about financial growth but about spreading happiness with every scoop of ice cream. His journey reminds us that behind every great achievement lies a story of struggles, sacrifices, and unwavering determination.

As we Savor the sweet success of Old Mumbai Ice Creams, let it inspire us to dream big, work hard, and carve our own path to greatness.

CHAPTER SIXTEEN

CHAPTER:15 MY SUCCESS STORY

Success, for me, has never been about luck—it's about vision, relentless effort, and the courage to take risks. When I founded Aritra Visual Studio, I had no idea how far it could go, but I was determined to create something meaningful. In just 1.5 years, my firm has not only generated ₹35 lakhs but has also taught me invaluable lessons about responsibility, innovation, and the power of perseverance. Balancing my entrepreneurial journey with my roles at Maa Tara Jewellers and my responsibilities as Deputy Technical CEO in the Student Council has been both challenging and rewarding. At Maa Tara Jewellers, I oversee marketing and technical operations, ensuring our family's legacy grows stronger with time. These experiences have shaped my understanding of teamwork, strategy, and leadership—qualities that are now the cornerstone of everything I do. But my journey is not just about business; it's about impact. Writing my debut book, "From Dreams to Riches: Inspiring Journeys of Indian Entrepreneurs," was my way of giving back. Through this book, I wanted to share stories of resilience and determination, hoping to inspire readers to believe in their own dreams, no matter how distant they may seem. Looking back, I see every challenge as a stepping stone. The journey hasn't been easy, but it has been incredibly fulfilling. Each milestone has strengthened my resolve to aim higher, to innovate, and to create opportunities not just for myself, but for others as well. My story is still being written, and I'm excited for the chapters yet to come

Conclusion: The Power of Human Potential

The journey of Indian entrepreneurs, from humble beginnings to extraordinary achievements, is a testament to the immense power of human potential. These visionary individuals have shown us that with grit, determination, and an unwavering belief in their dreams, remarkable things can happen. Their stories are not just about business success but also about resilience, overcoming adversity, and relentlessly pursuing a vision that often seemed impossible at the outset. These entrepreneurs have shaped industries, created jobs, and contributed significantly to India's economic growth, both locally and globally. They have proven time and again that the power of human potential, when harnessed, knows no bounds. As we have explored throughout this book, several key factors have played a pivotal role in the success of these entrepreneurs:

1. A Strong Entrepreneurial Spirit

The foundation of every successful entrepreneur is a deeprooted entrepreneurial spirit. This spirit is characterized by a relentless drive to take risks, innovate, and push the boundaries of what is possible. It is about thinking beyond the conventional, seeking opportunities where others see obstacles, and never settling for mediocrity. The entrepreneurial mindset fosters creativity, helping individuals come up with groundbreaking ideas that can revolutionize entire industries.

2. Adaptability and Resilience

In a rapidly changing world, the ability to adapt is critical to long-term success. Entrepreneurs must navigate dynamic market forces, technological advancements, and societal shifts. Resilience—the ability to bounce back from setbacks and learn from failures—is equally important. Many successful entrepreneurs have faced obstacles, from financial crises to personal losses, but their ability to adapt, pivot, and rise again has been a defining characteristic of their journeys. They view failure as a stepping stone, learning valuable lessons that fuel their future success.

3. Focus on Customer Needs

A true entrepreneurial leader always keeps the customer at the centre of their strategy. Successful entrepreneurs understand that the key to sustainable growth lies in identifying and addressing the needs of their customers. By prioritizing customer satisfaction, building strong relationships, and continuously delivering value, they are able to cultivate brand loyalty, drive word-of-mouth marketing, and stay ahead of competitors. Listening to customer feedback, anticipating market trends, and offering innovative solutions are all integral components of a customer-centric approach.

4. Building Strong Teams

No entrepreneur achieves success alone. Building a strong, reliable team is essential to achieving scale and long-term success. The best entrepreneurs recognize the value of hiring talented individuals who bring diverse skills, ideas, and perspectives. They create an environment that fosters collaboration, innovation, and personal growth. By empowering their teams, encouraging creativity, and providing opportunities for professional development, these entrepreneurs inspire loyalty, drive, and excellence among their employees.

5. Leveraging Technology

In today's digital age, technology is a powerful enabler of business success. Successful entrepreneurs leverage the latest technologies to streamline operations, enhance customer experiences, and drive innovation. Whether it is through data analytics, e-commerce platforms, artificial intelligence, or automation tools, technology allows businesses to scale quickly, improve efficiency, and offer superior products and services. Entrepreneurs who embrace technology stay ahead of the curve, continually evolving their business models to meet the changing demands of the market.

6. Ethical Business Practices

In an increasingly transparent world, ethical business practices are crucial for long-term sustainability. Successful entrepreneurs understand the importance of operating with integrity, fairness, and responsibility. By adhering to ethical principles and prioritizing social responsibility, they build trust with customers, partners, and employees. Ethical entrepreneurs understand that business success is not just about profit but also about contributing positively to society, supporting communities, and fostering a culture of trust and respect. This commitment to ethics not only ensures long-term success but also contributes to building a more equitable and just society.

7. Vision and Purpose

Finally, what sets many successful entrepreneurs apart is their unwavering sense of vision and purpose. They are driven by a clear sense of why they do what they do—a purpose that goes beyond monetary gain. Whether it is to solve a particular problem, make a positive impact on society, or create a legacy, entrepreneurs who are furled by purpose tend to stay motivated and focused, even when faced with adversity. Their vision provides clarity and direction, helping them navigate the inevitable ups and downs of the entrepreneurial journey. By understanding these factors and drawing inspiration from the stories of successful Indian entrepreneurs, aspiring entrepreneurs can embark on their own journeys toward realizing their dreams. The road to success is rarely smooth or straight. It is filled with challenges, setbacks, and moments of doubt. But it is also filled with opportunities, lessons, and moments of triumph. The key to navigating this journey is perseverance, passion, and the right mindset. With these tools in hand, anything is possible. Entrepreneurs must believe in themselves, them ideas, and their ability to overcome any obstacles that come their way. As we look ahead to the future, the power of human potential will

continue to drive innovation, shape industries, and transform the world. The next generation of Indian entrepreneurs is ready to take on the world, armed with the lessons learned from those who have paved the way before them. Their stories will inspire even greater achievements, and the cycle of entrepreneurship will continue, pushing the boundaries of what is possible and helping to build a better, more prosperous world for all

The Power Of Persistence

As we've seen through the stories of these incredible entrepreneurs, the most consistent thread that connects them all is their persistence. Each of them faced setbacks, challenges, and moments where quitting seemed like the easiest option. But they pushed through. They believed that failure wasn't the end but merely a stepping stone on the road to success.

Persistence is the engine that drives every entrepreneur forward. It is the force that keeps you going when things get tough, when the world seems against you, and when success feels like a distant dream. And while talent, ideas, and connections are important, persistence—especially when it feels like everything is working against you—separates the dreamers from the achievers.

Key Takeaway:

Success is not guaranteed, but your ability to persist is what sets you apart. When you find yourself in a struggle, remember, it's not the end; it's just the beginning of the next chapter.

Impact Beyond Wealth

In the end, success isn't only measured by how much money you make or the awards you receive. The true measure of success is the impact you have on the world around you. The entrepreneurs in this book did not just build businesses—they changed lives, improved communities, and inspired the next generation of dreamers and doers.

We live in a time where it's not enough to just make a profit. True leaders understand the responsibility that comes with success. They use their platforms to make a difference, to uplift others, and to contribute to a larger purpose. Whether it's through creating jobs, promoting sustainability, or investing in education, the future of business lies in the hands of those who understand that impact is the true currency.

Key Takeaway:

The wealth you accumulate is important, but the legacy you leave behind, the lives you touch, and the difference you make in the world will outlast any business venture. Make it count

The Journey Ahead

As we come to the end of this book, we find ourselves not at a conclusion, but at the beginning of something even greater. The journeys shared within these pages are not just stories; they are lessons, struggles, triumphs, and inspirations for anyone who dreams of making their mark in the world.

> *"Dreams are the seeds of future reality. The path to realizing them might be long and tough, but every step is worth it if you're building a future you're proud of." – Aritra Manna*

From dreams to riches, these entrepreneurs have shown us that the path to success is never straightforward, but it is always worth walking. Their resilience, vision, and unwavering determination are the bedrock upon which the future is being built. It is a reminder that success isn't about the destination; it's about the courage to start and the persistence to keep going, even when the odds are stacked against you.

While this book concludes with these stories, the journey doesn't end here. It extends into your hands, your heart, and your future. Whether you're at the start of your entrepreneurial journey or somewhere along the way, take these stories with you—let them guide you, challenge you, and inspire you to reach higher.

As you step forward, remember that the road to riches isn't just measured in wealth. True success is about the impact you make, the lives you touch, and the legacy you create.

The Future is Yours to Build.

Stay inspired. Keep dreaming. And never stop reaching for greatness.

If the response to this book is as overwhelming as we hope, stay tuned for Part 2, where we dive deeper into the new wave of entrepreneurs leading change across the globe.